MW00779998

Anti-Inflammatory

Diet

Cookbook

50+ No-Stress Recipes With Easy Ingredients To Heal The Immune System

Miriam Boonen

TABLE OF CONTENTS

INTRODUCTION:

A healthy diet is important for both your physical and mental health. Using a good diet will help you to maintain your weight and improve your overall health. This is why it is highly recommended that everyone should adopt an anti-inflammatory diet.

This movement has been around for a long time. Researchers have found out that eating a diet high in fat and cholesterol may result in the production of inflammation. This happens because many of your normal metabolic processes may be disrupted when you follow an anti-inflammatory diet.

There are many benefits associated with following this type of diet. For starters, this will help you to maintain a healthy weight, improve your skin condition, and reduce your risk of heart disease, diabetes, and cancer. Making sure that you have a balanced diet is always key to maintaining good health. This is especially true if you are going through any type of recovery or body building program.

"Anti-inflammatory diet is a 100% safe and tested weight loss program. It has been designed by dietitians with the help of nutritionists to help you reduce your weight. The ingredients that are used in this book are good for your body and have no harmful effect on it. It provides you a good variety of recipes that you need to follow them at every step of your dieting process."

For most people, the ideal diet is a balance of nutritious, fiber-rich foods and low-calorie, low-sodium meals. Those who have chronic inflammatory bowel disease (IBD) or other conditions that cause inflammation may also benefit from a low-inflammatory diet.

A low-inflammatory diet has an abundance of healthy fats and foods rich in fiber. For most people with IBD, it's also important to limit the load of sugars and simple carbohydrates. In addition to that, a person should choose moderate amounts of protein and consume several servings daily of fruits and vegetables for optimal nutrition. These dietary changes can help you lose weight, feel healthier and improve your overall quality of life.

For most people, the ideal diet is a balance of nutritious, fiber-rich foods and low-calorie, low-sodium meals. Those who have chronic inflammatory bowel disease (IBD) or other conditions that cause inflammation may also benefit from a low-inflammatory diet. A low-inflammatory diet has an abundance of healthy fats and foods rich in fiber. For most people with IBD, it's also important to limit the load of sugars and simple carbohydrates. In addition to that, a person should choose moderate amounts of protein and consume several servings daily of fruits and vegetables for optimal nutrition. These dietary changes can help you lose weight, feel healthier and improve your overall quality of life.

BREAKFAST

1. Pumpkin Quinoa Porridge

Preparation Time: 2 minutes

Cooking Time: 1 minute

Servings: 4

Ingredients:

- ¾ cup dry quinoa
- 2 cups water
- ¾ cup pumpkin purée
- ¼ cup monk fruit sweetener
- 1½ teaspoons pumpkin pie spice
- 1 teaspoon pure vanilla extract
- ¼ teaspoon salt

Directions:

1. Using a fine-mesh strainer, rinse the quinoa very well until the water runs clear.
2. Add the quinoa, water, pumpkin purée, sweetener, pumpkin pie spice, vanilla, and salt to the inner pot. Stir to combine. Secure the lid.
3. Press the Manual or Pressure Cook button and adjust the time to 1 minute.
4. When the timer beeps, quick-release pressure until float valve drops and then unlock lid.
5. Allow the quinoa to cool slightly before spooning into bowls to serve.

Nutrition: Calories: 141 Fat: 2g Protein: 5g Sodium: 148mg Fiber: 3g Carbohydrates: 37g Sugar: 2g

2. Pumpkin Is For More than Just Pie

Preparation Time: 5 minutes

Cooking Time: 5 minutes

Servings: 4

Ingredients:

- 2 cups old fashioned rolled oats
- 1 teaspoon baking powder
- 2 tablespoons erythritol
- 1 tablespoon poppy seeds
- ¼ teaspoon salt
- 1 large egg
- Juice and zest from 1 Meyer lemon
- 1 cup unsweetened vanilla almond milk

Directions:

1. Lightly grease four (8-ounce) ramekin dishes. Set aside.
2. In a medium bowl, mix together the oats, baking powder, erythritol, poppy seeds, and salt. Add the egg, juice and zest from the lemon, and the almond milk and stir to combine. Divide the oatmeal mixture into the four dishes.
3. Pour ½ cup water into the inner pot of the Instant Pot®. Place the steam rack inside the inner pot and place the ramekins on top of the rack. Secure the lid.
4. Press the Manual or Pressure Cook button and adjust the time to 5 minutes.
5. When the timer beeps, quick-release pressure until float valve drops and then unlock lid.

6. The ramekins will be hot when you open the lid, so be sure to use your mini oven mitts to lift them out of the Instant Pot® and let them cool before serving.

Nutrition: Calories: 229 Fat,: 6g Protein: 9g Sodium: 330mg Fiber: 9g Carbohydrates: 40g | Sugar: 1g

3. Apple Cinnamon Steel Cut Oats

Preparation Time: 10 minutes

Cooking Time: 4 minutes

Servings: 6

Ingredients:

- 2 cups steel cut oats
- 3 cups unsweetened vanilla almond milk
- 3 cups water
- 3 small apples, peeled, cored, and cut into 1"-thick chunks
- 2 teaspoons ground cinnamon
- ¼ cup date syrup
- ¼ teaspoon salt

Directions:

1. Add the steel cut oats, almond milk, water, apple chunks, cinnamon, date syrup, and salt to the Instant Pot® and stir to combine. Secure the lid.
2. Press the Manual or Pressure Cook button and adjust the time to 4 minutes.
3. When the timer beeps, let pressure release naturally for 15 minutes, then quick-release any remaining pressure until float valve drops, then unlock lid.
4. Serve warm.

Nutrition: Calories: 311 Fat,: 6g Protein: 10g Sodium: 193mg Fiber: 8g Carbohydrates: 57g Sugar: 15g

4. Triple Berry Steel Cut Oats

Preparation Time: 5 minutes

Cooking Time: 4 minutes

Servings: 6

Ingredients:

- 2 cups steel cut oats
- 3 cups unsweetened almond milk
- 3 cups water
- 1 teaspoon pure vanilla extract
- 1/3 cup monk fruit sweetener
- ¼ teaspoon salt
- 1½ cups frozen berry blend with strawberries, blackberries, and raspberries

Directions:

1. Add the steel cut oats, almond milk, water, vanilla, sweetener, and salt to the Instant Pot® and stir to combine. Place the frozen berries on top. Secure the lid.
2. Press the Manual or Pressure Cook button on the Instant Pot® and adjust the time to 4 minutes.
3. When the timer beeps, let pressure release naturally for 15 minutes, then quick-release any remaining pressure until float valve drops, then unlock lid. Serve warm.

Nutrition: Calories: 262 Fat: 6g Protein: 10g Sodium: 187mg Fiber: 9g Carbohydrates: 55g | Sugar: 3g

5. Banana Pancake Bites

Preparation Time: 10 minutes

Cooking Time: 6 minutes

Servings: 3

Ingredients:

- 1¾ cups old fashioned rolled oats
- 3 small ripe bananas
- 3 large eggs
- 2 tablespoons erythritol
- 1 teaspoon ground cinnamon
- 1 teaspoon pure vanilla extract
- 1 teaspoon baking powder

Directions:

1. Place the oats, bananas, eggs, erythritol, cinnamon, vanilla, and baking powder in a large, powerful blender and blend until very smooth, about 1 minute.
2. Pour the mixture into a silicone mold with seven wells. Place a paper towel on top and then top with aluminum foil. Tighten the edges to prevent extra moisture getting inside. Place the mold on top of your steam rack with handles.
3. Pour 1 cup water into the inner pot. Place the steam rack and mold inside. Secure the lid.
4. Press the Manual or Pressure Cook button and adjust the time to 6 minutes.
5. When the timer beeps, quick-release pressure until float valve drops and then unlock lid.

6. Pull the steam rack and mold out of the Instant Pot® and remove the aluminum foil and paper towel. Allow the pancake bites to cool completely, and then use a knife to pull the edges of the bites away from the mold. Press on the bottom of the mold and the pancake bites will pop right out.

Nutrition: Calories: 389 Fat: 9g Protein: 16g Sodium: 234mg Fiber: 9g Carbohydrates: 70g | Sugar: 14g

6. Cinnamon Flaxseed Breakfast Loaf

Preparation Time: 10 minutes

Cooking Time: 30 minutes

Servings: 6

Ingredients:

- ½ cup ground golden flaxseed meal
- ½ cup almond flour
- 1 tablespoon ground cinnamon
- 2 teaspoons baking powder
- ½ teaspoon salt
- 2/3 cup xylitol
- 4 large eggs
- ½ cup coconut oil, melted and cooled

Directions:

1. In a medium bowl, whisk together the flaxseed meal, flour, cinnamon, baking powder, salt, and xylitol.
2. In a separate medium bowl, whisk together the eggs and cooled coconut oil. Pour the wet ingredients into the dry ingredients and stir to combine.
3. Grease a 6" cake pan well and pour the mixture into the pan and cover with aluminum foil.
4. Pour 1½ cups water into the inner pot and place the steam rack with handles in the pot. Place the cake pan on top of the steam rack. Secure the lid.
5. Press the Manual or Pressure Cook button and adjust the time to 30 minutes.

6. When the timer beeps, quick-release pressure until float valve drops and then unlock lid. Carefully remove the pan from the Instant Pot® and allow the bread to cool completely before flipping the pan upside down and removing the loaf. Slice and serve.

Nutrition: Calories: 389 Fat,: 30g Protein: 9g Sodium: 407mg Fiber: 6g Carbohydrates: 29g Sugar: 1g

7. Root Vegetable Egg Casserole

Preparation Time: 10 minutes

Cooking Time: 29 minutes

Servings: 4

Ingredients:

- 1 tablespoon avocado oil
- 1 small yellow onion, peeled and diced
- 1 small turnip, peeled and diced
- 1 medium parsnip, peeled and diced
- 2 small carrots, peeled and diced
- 1 teaspoon kosher salt
- 8 large eggs
- 1 tablespoon lemon juice
- 1 tablespoon fresh thyme leaves

Directions:

1. Add the oil to the inner pot and press the Sauté button. Allow the oil to heat 1 minute and then add the onion, turnip, parsnip, carrots, and salt. Cook until the vegetables are softened, 10 minutes. Press the Cancel button.
2. In a medium bowl, whisk together the eggs and lemon juice. Add the thyme and vegetable mixture and stir to combine.
3. Spray the inside of a 7-cup glass bowl with cooking spray. Transfer the egg mixture to the bowl.

4. Add 1 cup water to the inner pot and place the steam rack inside. Place the bowl on top of the steam rack. Secure the lid.
5. Press the Manual or Pressure Cook button and adjust the time to 18 minutes.
6. When the timer beeps, quick-release pressure until float valve drops and then unlock lid.
7. Remove bowl from pot and allow to cool 5 minutes before slicing and serving.

Nutrition: Calories: 221 Fat: 12g Protein: 14g Sodium: 754mg Fiber: 3g Carbohydrates: 12g Sugar: 5g

8. Strawberries and Cream Quinoa Porridge

Preparation Time: 2 minutes

Cooking Time: 1 minute

Servings: 6

Ingredients:

- 1½ cups dry quinoa
- 1½ cups water
- 1 (13.66-ounce) can unsweetened full-fat coconut milk
- ½ teaspoon pure stevia powder
- 1 teaspoon pure vanilla extract
- 1 cup sliced strawberries
- 1/3 cup unsweetened shredded coconut

Directions:

1. Using a fine-mesh strainer, rinse the quinoa very well until the water runs clear.
2. Add the quinoa, water, coconut milk, stevia, and vanilla to the inner pot. Stir to combine. Secure the lid.
3. Press the Manual or Pressure Cook button and adjust the time to 1 minute.
4. When the timer beeps, quick-release pressure until float valve drops and then unlock lid.
5. Stir in strawberries. Allow the quinoa to cool slightly before spooning into bowls to serve. Top each bowl with a portion of the coconut.

Nutrition: Calories: 323 Fat: 18g Protein: 8g Sodium: 10mg Fiber: 4g Carbohydrates: 32g Sugar: 2g

9. Egg Casserole with Kale

Preparation Time: 10 minutes

Cooking Time: 17 minutes

Servings: 6

Ingredients:

- 1 tablespoon avocado oil
- 1 small yellow onion, peeled and chopped
- 5 large kale leaves, tough stems removed and finely chopped
- 1 clove garlic, diced
- 2 tablespoons lemon juice
- ½ teaspoon salt, divided
- 9 large eggs
- 2 tablespoons water
- 1½ teaspoons dried rosemary
- 1 teaspoon dried oregano
- ¼ teaspoon black pepper
- ½ cup nutritional yeast

Directions:

1. Add the oil to the pot, press the Sauté button and heat oil for 1 minute.
2. Add the onion and sauté 2 minutes until just softened.
3. Add the kale, garlic, lemon juice, and ¼ teaspoon salt. Stir and allow to cook 2 minutes more. Press the Cancel button.

4. Meanwhile, in a medium bowl, whisk together the eggs, water, rosemary, oregano, ¼ teaspoon salts, pepper, and nutritional yeast.
5. Add the onion and kale mixture to the egg mixture and stir to combine.
6. Rinse the inner pot, add 2 cups water, and place a steam rack inside.
7. Spray a 7" spring form pan with cooking spray. Transfer the egg mixture to the spring form pan.
8. Place the pan on the steam rack and secure the lid. Press the Manual or Pressure Cook button and adjust time to 12 minutes.
9. When the timer beeps, quick-release pressure until float valve drops and then unlock lid.
10. Remove the pan from pot and allow to cool 5 minutes before slicing and serving.

Nutrition: Calories: 157 Fat: 9g Protein: 13g Sodium: 311mg Fiber: 2g Carbohydrates: 5g Sugar: 1g

LUNCH

10. Kale Salad

Preparation Time: 10 minutes

Cooking Time: 30 minutes

Servings: 6

Ingredients:

- 2 Tablespoons Apple Cider Vinegar
- 1 Teaspoon Sea Salt, Fine
- ½ Teaspoon Red Pepper Flakes
- ¼ Teaspoon Black Pepper
- 2 Sweet Potatoes Small & Peeled
- 1 Leek, Small
- 1 Apple, Peeled
- ¼ Cup Pine Nuts
- 1 Tablespoon Avocado Oil
- 3 Tablespoons Olive Oil
- 15 Ounces Kale, Stemmed & Chopped

Directions:

1. Start by heating your oven to 350.
2. Get out a baking sheet, and line it with parchment paper.
3. Combine your kale, olive oil, red pepper flakes, black pepper and vinegar. Knead these spices and oil into your kale for a minute. Transfer three quarters of this mixture to your baking pan, spreading it out. Bake for

twenty minutes, tossing halfway through. Add it back to your remaining kale.

4. Chop your leeks, sweet potatoes, and apple into bite sized pieces, and then throw your avocado oil in a skillet. Place your skillet over medium heat, cooking the mixture for ten minutes. Your sweet potatoes should be soft.

5. Remove the kale from the oven, and then top your sweet potato mixture with it and pine nuts. Mix well before serving.

Nutrition: Calories: 213 Protein: 5 Grams Fat: 14 Grams Carbs: 22 Grams

11. Spicy Ramen Soup

Preparation Time: 10 minutes

Cooking Time: 15 minutes

Servings: 4

Ingredients:

- 2 Tablespoons Sesame Seeds
- 8 Ounces Rice Noodles, Cooked
- ¼ Cup Cucumber, Sliced Thin
- ¼ Cup Scallion, Sliced
- ¼ Cup Cilantro, Fresh & chopped
- 2 Tablespoons Sesame Oil
- 1 Tablespoon Coconut Aminos
- 1 Tablespoon Ginger, Fresh, Grated & Peeled
- 2 Tablespoons Rice vinegar
- 1 Tablespoons Honey, Raw
- 1 Tablespoon Lime Juice, Fresh
- 1 Teaspoon Chili Powder

Directions:

1. Mix your sesame seeds, cucumber, scallion, noodles, cilantro, sesame oil, ginger, coconut aminos, vinegar, honey, chili powder and lime juice together.
2. Dive amount four soup bowls, and serve at room temperature.

Nutrition: Calories: 663 Protein: 21 Grams Fat: 28 Grams Carbs: 115 Grams

12. Miso Soup with Greens

Preparation Time: 10 minutes

Cooking Time: 15 minutes

Servings: 4

Ingredients:

- 3 Cups Water
- 4 Scallions, Sliced Thin
- 3 Cups Vegetable Broth
- ½ Teaspoon Fish Sauce
- 1 Cup Mushrooms, Sliced
- 3 Tablespoons Miso Paste
- 1 Cup Baby Spinach, Fresh & Washed

Directions:

1. Get out a soup pot, placing it over high heat. Add in your fish sauce, water, broth, and mushrooms. Bring it to a boil before taking it off of heat.
2. Mix your miso paste and a half a cup of your broth together until the miso paste dissolves. Stir this mixture back into the soup.
3. Stir in your scallions and spinach, serving warm.

Nutrition: Calories: 44 Protein: 2 Grams Fat: 0 Grams Carbs: 8 Grams

13. Chicken Chili

Preparation Time: 10 minutes

Cooking Time: 30 minutes

Servings: 4

Ingredients:

- 8 Ounce Can Green Chilies, Mild, Diced & With Liquid
- 4 Cups White Beans, Cooked & Drained
- 4 Cups Chicken Broth
- 4 Teaspoon Cumin, Ground
- 1 Teaspoon Chili Powder
- 2 Teaspoon Oregano, Dried
- 4 Cups Chicken, Shredded & Cooked
- ¼ Teaspoon Cayenne Pepper
- 2 Scallions, Sliced
- 1 Tablespoon Ghee
- 6 Cloves Garlic, Minced
- 2 Onions, Small & Chopped
- 1 Tablespoon Ghee

Directions:

1. Get out a soup pot, placing it over medium heat. Melt your ghee in it before adding your garlic and onion in. sauté for five minutes, stirring well.

2. Add in your chilies, cooking for another two minutes. Remember to stir.

3. Stir in your oregano, chili, cayenne, cumin, beans and broth. Bring the mixture to a simmer.

4. Add in your chicken, letting it come to a simmer again. Reduce the heat to medium-low, and cook for another ten minutes.
5. Top with scallions before serving warm.

Nutrition: Calories: 304 Protein: 21 Grams Fat: 4 Grams Carbs: 46 Grams

14. Lentil Stew

Preparation Time: 10minutes

Cooking Time: 30 minutes

Servings: 4

Ingredients:

- 1 Tablespoon Olive Oil
- 8 Brussels Sprouts, Halved
- 3 Carrots, Peeled & Sliced
- 1 Onion, Chopped
- 1 Turnip, Peeled, Quartered & Sliced
- 6 Cups Vegetable Broth
- 1 Clove Garlic, Sliced
- 15 Ounce Can Lentils, Drained & Rinsed
- 1 Cup Corn, Frozen
- 1 Tablespoon Parsley, Fresh & Chopped
- Sea Salt & Black Pepper to Taste

Directions:

1. Get out a Dutch oven and heat your oil over high heat, adding in your onion. Cook for three minutes. Your onions should soften.
2. Add in your carrots, turnip, garlic, and Brussels sprouts. Cook for three more minutes.
3. Throw in your broth, bringing it to a boil. Once it boils, reduce it to a simmer. Cook for five more minutes or until your vegetables are tender.

4. Add in your salt, pepper, parsley, corn and lentils. Cook enough for everything to heat all the way through, and serve warm.

Nutrition: Calories: 240 Protein: 10 Grams Fat: 4 Grams Carbs: 42 Grams

DINNER

15. Zucchini and Lemon Herb Salmon

Preparation Time: 15 minutes

Cooking Time: 20 minutes

Servings: 4

Ingredients:

- 2 tablespoons of olive oil
- 4 chopped zucchinis
- 2 tablespoons of lemon juice
- 2 tablespoons of agave nectar
- 2 garlic cloves, minced
- 1 tablespoon of Dijon mustard
- ½ teaspoon oregano, dried
- ½ teaspoon dill, dried
- ¼ teaspoon rosemary, dried
- ¼ teaspoon thyme, dried
- 4 salmon fillets
- 2 tablespoons parsley leaves, chopped
- Ground black pepper and kosher salt to taste

Directions:

1. Preheat your oven to 400 degrees F.
2. Apply cooking spray on your baking sheet lightly.
3. Whisk together the lemon juice, brown sugar, dill, garlic, Dijon, rosemary, thyme, and oregano in a bowl.
4. Season with pepper and salt to taste. Set aside.

5. Keep the zucchini on your baking sheet in one single layer.
6. Drizzle some olive oil. Season with pepper and salt.
7. Add the fish in one layer. Brush each fillet with your herb mix.
8. Keep in the oven. Cook for 17 minutes.
9. Garnish with parsley and serve.

Nutrition: Calories 355 Carbohydrates 15g Cholesterol 78mg Total Fat 19g Protein 31g Sugar 12g Fiber 2g Sodium 132mg

16. Parmesan and Lemon Fish

Preparation Time: 15 minutes

Cooking Time: 10 minutes

Servings: 2

Ingredients:

- 4 tilapia fillets
- ¼ cup cornflakes, crushed
- 2 tablespoons of vegan Parmesan, grated
- 2 teaspoons vegan dairy-free butter, melted
- 1/8 teaspoon black pepper, ground
- ½ teaspoon lemon peel, shredded
- Lemon wedges

Directions:

1. Heat your oven to 450 ℉.
2. Rinse and then dry the fish using paper towels.
3. Apply cooking spray on your baking pan.
4. Now roll up your fish fillets. Start from their short ends.
5. Keep in the baking pan.
6. Bring together the vegan butter, Parmesan, corn flakes, pepper and lemon peel in a bowl.
7. Sprinkle the crumb mix on your fish roll-ups.
8. Press the crumbs lightly into the fish.
9. Bake for 6-8 minutes. The fish should flake easily with your fork.
10. Serve with lemon wedges.

Nutrition: Calories 191 Cholesterol 71mg Carbohydrates 7g Fat 7g Sugar 1g Fiber 0g Protein 25g

17. Chicken Lemon Piccata

Preparation Time: 10 minutes

Cooking Time: 20 minutes

Servings: 4

Ingredients:

- 2 chicken breasts, skinless & boneless
- 2 tablespoons dairy-free margarine
- 1-1/2 tablespoons whole wheat flour
- ¼ teaspoon salt
- ¼ teaspoon white pepper
- 1/3 cup white wine, dry
- 2 tablespoons olive oil
- ¼ cup lemon juice
- 1/3 cup chicken stock, low-sodium
- ¼ cup minced Italian parsley
- ¼ cup capers, drained
- Pepper and salt to taste

Directions:

1. Cut in half each chicken breast.
2. Spread your flour on a plate thinly. Season with pepper and salt.
3. Dredge the breast slices lightly in your seasoned flour. Set aside.
4. Heat your sauté pan over medium temperature.
5. Add the breast slices to your pan when you see the oil simmering.
6. Cook for 3 to 4 minutes.

7. Turn over the chicken slices.

8. Take out the slices. Set aside.

9. Add wine to the pan. Stir. Scrape up those browned bits from the bottom.

10. Now add the chicken stock and lemon juice.

11. Go to high heat. Boil till you have a thick sauce.

12. Bring down the heat. Stir the parsley and capers in.

13. Add back the breast slices to your pan. Rewarm.

Nutrition: Calories 227 Cholesterol 72mg Carbohydrates 3g Fat 15g Fiber 1g Sugar 0g Protein 20g

18. Blackened Chicken Breast

Preparation Time: 10 minutes

Cooking Time: 15 minutes

Servings: 2

Ingredients:

- 2 chicken breast halves, skinless and boneless
- 1 teaspoon thyme, ground
- 2 teaspoons of paprika
- 2 teaspoons olive oil
- ½ teaspoon onion powder

Directions:

1. Combine the thyme, paprika, onion powder, and salt together in your bowl.
2. Transfer the spice mix to a flat plate.
3. Rub olive oil on the chicken breast. Coat fully.
4. Roll the chicken pieces in the spice mixture. Press down, ensuring that all sides have the spice mix.
5. Keep aside for 5 minutes.
6. In the meantime, preheat your air fryer to 360 degrees F.
7. Keep the chicken in the air fryer basket. Cook for 8 minutes.
8. Flip once and cook for another 7 minutes.
9. Transfer the breasts to a serving plate. Serve after 5 minutes.

Nutrition: Calories 424 Carbohydrates 3g Cholesterol 198mg Total Fat 11g Protein 79g Sugar 1g Fiber 2g Sodium 516mg

19. Chicken Marrakesh

Preparation Time: 25 minutes

Cooking Time: 4 hours

Servings: 8

Ingredients:

- 1 slice onion
- 2 garlic cloves, minced
- ½ lb. pumpkins
- 2 carrots, diced & peeled
- 1 lb. garbanzo beans, drained & rinsed
- ½ teaspoon cumin, ground
- 2 lbs. chicken breasts, skinless, halved, cut into small pieces
- ¼ teaspoon cinnamon, ground
- ½ teaspoon turmeric, ground
- ½ teaspoon black pepper, ground
- 1 teaspoon salt
- 1 teaspoon parsley, dried
- ½ lb. tamarind, pulped

Directions:

1. Keep the garlic, onion, pumpkin, carrots, chicken breast and garbanzo beans in your slow cooker.
2. Mix turmeric, cumin, black pepper, cinnamon, salt and parsley in your bowl.
3. Sprinkle over the vegetables and chicken.
4. Add the tamarind. Combine well by stirring.
5. Keep your cooker covered. Set the heat to high.

6. Cook for 4 hours. The sauce should be thick.

Nutrition: Calories 520 Carbohydrates 59g Cholesterol 101mg Fat 15g Fiber 13g Sugar 25g Protein 45g Sodium 424mg

20. Shrimp and Vegetable Curry

Preparation Time: 5 minutes

Cooking Time: 10 minutes

Servings: 4

Ingredients:

- 1 sliced onion
- 3 tablespoons of olive oil
- 2 teaspoons of curry powder
- 1 cup of coconut milk
- 1 cauliflower
- 1 lb. shrimp tails

Directions:

1. Add the onion to your oil.
2. Sauté to make it a bit soft.
3. Steam your vegetables in the meantime.
4. Add the curry seasoning, coconut milk, and spices if you want once the onion has become soft.
5. Cook for 2 minutes.
6. Include the shrimp. Cook for 5 minutes.
7. Serve with the steamed vegetables.

Nutrition: Calories 491 Carbohydrates 11g Cholesterol 208mg Fat 39g Protein 24g Sugar 3g Fiber 5g Sodium 309mg

SIDE DISHES

21. Baked Broccoli

Preparation time: 10 minutes

Cooking time: 30 minutes

Servings: 4

Ingredients:

- 2-pounds broccoli, roughly chopped
- 2 tablespoons olive oil
- 1 tablespoon cayenne pepper

Directions:

1. Line the baking tray with baking paper.
2. Put the broccoli in the tray and sprinkle with olive oil and cayenne pepper.
3. Bake the broccoli for 30 minutes at 355F.

Nutrition: 141 calories, 6.5g protein, 15.8g carbohydrates, 8g fat, 6.3g fiber, 0mg cholesterol, 75mg sodium, 745mg potassium.

22. Sweet Quinoa

Preparation time: 10 minutes

Cooking time: 20 minutes

Servings: 4

Ingredients:

- 1 cup pears, chopped
- 1 cup quinoa
- 3 cups of water
- 1 tablespoon almond butter

Directions:

1. Mix water with quinoa and cook it on low heat for 10 minutes.
2. Then add pears and almond butter. Stir the meal and cook it for 10 minutes.

Nutrition: 209 calories, 7.3g protein, 34.8g carbohydrates, 5g fat, 5g fiber, 0mg cholesterol, 40mg sodium, 316mg potassium.

23. Cayenne Pepper Green Beans

Preparation time: 10 minutes

Cooking time: 20 minutes

Servings: 4

Ingredients:

- 1 teaspoon cayenne pepper
- 1 pound green beans, trimmed and halved
- 1 tablespoon avocado oil
- 2 cups of water

Directions:

1. Bring the water to boil and add green beans. Cook them for 10 minutes.
2. Then remove water and add avocado oil and cayenne pepper.
3. Roast the vegetables for 2-3 minutes on high heat.

Nutrition: 41 calories, 2.2g protein, 8.5g carbohydrates, 0.7g fat, 4.1g fiber, 0mg cholesterol, 11mg sodium, 258mg potassium.

24. Lime Brussels Sprouts

Preparation time: 10 minutes

Cooking time: 20 minutes

Servings: 4

Ingredients:

- 2 pounds Brussels sprouts, trimmed and halved
- 1 tablespoon olive oil
- 2 tablespoons lime juice
- 1 teaspoon lime zest, grated
- 1 teaspoon ground paprika

Directions:

1. Mix Brussel sprouts with olive oil, lime juice, lime zest, and ground paprika.
2. Put the vegetables in the lined with the baking paper tray and bake for 20 minutes at 365F.

Nutrition: 130 calories, 7.8g protein, 21g carbohydrates, 4.3g fat, 8.8g fiber, 0mg cholesterol, 57mg sodium, 895mg potassium.

25. Cabbage Bowl

Preparation time: 10 minutes

Cooking time: 20 minutes

Servings: 4

Ingredients:

- 4 cups white cabbage
- 1 cup tomatoes, diced
- 2 tablespoons olive oil
- 2 cups of water
- 1 teaspoon dried parsley

Directions:

1. Mix white cabbage with tomatoes in the saucepan.
2. Add water, dried parsley, and olive oil.
3. Close the lid and simmer the meal on medium heat for 20 minutes.

Nutrition: 86 calories, 1.3g protein, 5.8g carbohydrates, 7.2g fat, 2.3g fiber, 0mg cholesterol, 19mg sodium, 229mg potassium.

26. Parmesan Asparagus

Preparation time: 10 minutes

Cooking time: 15 minutes

Servings: 4

Ingredients:

- 3 oz Parmesan, grated
- 2 tablespoons olive oil
- 1 bunch asparagus, trimmed and halved

Directions:

1. Line the baking tray with baking paper.
2. Put the asparagus in the tray in one layer and sprinkle it with Parmesan and olive oil.
3. Bake the asparagus at 385F for 15 minutes.

Nutrition: 142 calories, 8.3g protein, 3.4g carbohydrates, 11.6g fat, 1.4g fiber, 15mg cholesterol, 199mg sodium, 135mg potassium.

27. Coconut Quinoa

Preparation time: 10 minutes

Cooking time: 25 minutes

Servings: 4

Ingredients:

- 1 cup quinoa
- 2 cups of water
- 1 cup of coconut milk
- 1 teaspoon ground turmeric

Directions:

1. Mix water with quinoa and coconut milk.
2. Add ground turmeric and close cook the meal on low heat for 25 minutes.

Nutrition: 296 calories, 7.4g protein, 31g carbohydrates, 16.9g fat, 4.4g fiber, 0mg cholesterol, 15mg sodium, 412mg potassium.

28. Rosemary Black Beans

Preparation time: 10 minutes

Cooking time: 0 minutes

Servings: 4

Ingredients:

- 1 tablespoon avocado oil
- 2 cups canned black beans, drained and rinsed
- 1 tablespoon dried rosemary
- 1 tablespoon lemon juice
- 1 onion, sliced

Directions:

1. Mix black beans with dried rosemary and lemon juice.
2. Add onion and avocado oil. Shake the meal well.

Nutrition: 350 calories, 21.4g protein, 63.9g carbohydrates, 2g fat, 15.9g fiber, 0mg cholesterol, 7mg sodium, 1502mg potassium.

29. Oregano Green Beans

Preparation time: 10 minutes

Cooking time: 15 minutes

Servings: 4

Ingredients:

- 1 pound green beans, trimmed and halved
- 1 cup of water
- 1 tablespoon dried oregano
- 1 teaspoon chili powder
- 1 tablespoon almond butter

Directions:

1. Bring the water to boil.
2. Add green beans and boil them for 10 minutes.
3. Then transfer the green beans in the bowl and add dried oregano, chili powder, and almond butter.
4. Stir the meal well.

Nutrition: 65 calories, 3.1g protein, 9.9g carbohydrates, 2.6g fat, 5g fiber, 0mg cholesterol, 16mg sodium, 299mg potassium.

MEAT

30. Pork with Corn and Peas

Preparation Time: 10 minutes

Cooking Time: 40 minutes

Servings: 4

Ingredients:

- 2 pounds pork stew meat, cut into strips
- ½ cup corn
- ½ cup green peas
- 2 tablespoons olive oil
- ½ cup yellow onion, chopped
- 3 tablespoons coconut aminos
- ½ cup vegetable stock
- A pinch of salt and black pepper

Directions:

1. Heat up a pan with the oil over medium heat, add the meat and the onion and brown for 10 minutes.
2. Add the corn and the other ingredients, toss, cook over medium heat for 30 minutes more, divide between plates and serve.

Nutrition: calories 250, fat 4, fiber 6, carbs 9.7, protein 12

31. **Pork with Carrots**

Preparation Time: 10 minutes

Cooking Time: 1 hour

Servings: 4

Ingredients:

- 1 pound pork meat, cubed
- 2 carrots, sliced
- 2 tablespoons avocado oil
- 1 yellow onion, chopped
- A pinch of salt and black pepper
- ¼ teaspoon smoked paprika
- ½ cup tomato sauce

Directions:

1. Heat up a pan with the oil over medium-high heat, add the onion and the meat and brown for 10 minutes.
2. Add the rest of the ingredients, toss, put the pan in the oven and bake at 390 degrees F for 50 minutes.
3. Divide everything between plates and serve.

Nutrition: calories 300, fat 7, fiber 6, carbs 12, protein 20

32. Pork and Creamy Leeks

Preparation Time: 10 minutes

Cooking Time: 55 minutes

Servings: 4

Ingredients:

- 2 pounds pork stew meat, cubed
- 3 leeks, sliced
- 2 tablespoons olive oil
- 1 teaspoon black peppercorns
- 1 tablespoon parsley, chopped
- 2 cups coconut cream
- 1 teaspoon rosemary, dried
- A pinch of salt and black pepper

Directions:

1. Heat up a pan with the oil over medium heat, add the leeks and the meat and brown for 5 minutes.
2. Add the rest of the ingredients, toss, put the pan in the oven and bake at 390 degrees F for 50 minutes.
3. Divide everything into bowls and serve.

Nutrition: calories 280, fat 5, fiber 7, carbs 12, protein 18

33. Tarragon Pork Roast

Preparation Time: 10 minutes

Cooking Time: 1 hour

Servings: 4

Ingredients:

- 2 pounds pork loin roast, sliced
- 1 tablespoon tarragon, chopped
- A pinch of salt and black pepper
- 4 garlic cloves, chopped
- 1 teaspoon red pepper, crushed
- ¼ cup olive oil

Directions:

1. In a roasting pan, combine the roast with the tarragon and the other ingredients, toss and bake at 390 degrees F for 1 hour.
2. Divide the mix between plates and serve.

Nutrition: calories 281, fat 5, fiber 7, carbs 8, protein 10

34. Roast with Onions and Potatoes

Preparation Time: 10 minutes

Cooking Time: 1 hour

Servings: 4

Ingredients:

- 2 pounds pork roast, sliced
- 2 sweet potatoes, peeled and sliced
- 2 tablespoons olive oil
- 1 teaspoon rosemary, dried
- 1 teaspoon turmeric powder
- 2 yellow onions, sliced
- ½ cup veggie stock
- A pinch of salt and black pepper

Directions:

1. In a roasting pan, combine the pork slices with the sweet potatoes, the onions and the other ingredients, toss and bake at 400 degrees F for 1 hours.
2. Divide everything between plates and serve.

Nutrition: calories 290, fat 4, fiber 7, carbs 10, protein 17

35. Pork with Pineapple and Mango

Preparation Time: 10 minutes

Cooking Time: 40 minutes

Servings: 4

Ingredients:

- 4 pork chops
- 2 tablespoons olive oil
- ½ cup vegetable stock
- 4 scallions, chopped
- 1 cup pineapple, peeled and cubed
- 1 mango, peeled and cubed
- 4 tablespoons lime juice
- 1 handful basil, chopped
- A pinch of salt and cayenne pepper

Directions:

1. Heat up a pan with the oil over medium heat, add the scallions and the meat and brown for 5 minutes.
2. Add the pineapple and the other ingredients, toss, cook over medium heat for 35 minutes more, divide between plates and serve.

Nutrition: calories 250, fat 5, fiber 6, carbs 8, protein 17

36. Pork with Celery and Sprouts

Preparation Time: 10 minutes

Cooking Time: 40 minutes

Servings: 4

Ingredients:

- 2 pounds pork stew meat, roughly cubed
- 2 tablespoons olive oil
- 2 tablespoons lemon juice
- 5 garlic cloves, minced
- 2 stalks celery, chopped
- 1 cup Brussels sprouts, trimmed and halved
- A pinch of salt and black pepper
- ½ teaspoon cinnamon powder
- 2 tablespoons parsley, chopped

Directions:

1. Heat up a pan with the oil over medium-high heat, add the garlic and the meat and brown for 5 minutes.
2. Add the celery and the other ingredients, toss, introduce the pan in the oven and cook at 400 degrees F for 35 minutes more.
3. Divide the mix between plates and serve.

Nutrition: calories 284, fat 4, fiber 4, carbs 9, protein 15

37. Smoked Beef Sausage Bake with Broccoli

Preparation Time: 45 minutes

Cooking Time: 40 minutes

Servings: 4

Ingredients

- 1 red bell pepper, thinly sliced
- 2 shallots, chopped
- 1 cup broccoli, broken into florets
- 4 smoked beef sausages, sliced
- 1 green bell pepper, thinly sliced
- 2 tablespoons fresh parsley, roughly chopped
- 2 garlic cloves, minced
- 1/2 teaspoon ground bay leaf
- Salt and black pepper, to taste
- 1 teaspoon marjoram
- 6 eggs, whisked

Directions

1. Begin by preheating your oven to 3700F.
2. Heat up a nonstick skillet using a moderate flame; now, Heat the sausage for 3 minutes, stirring regularly.
3. Include the peppers, shallots, broccoli, and garlic; continue cooking for about 5 minutes. Season with marjoram, salt, pepper and ground bay leaf.
4. Move the sausage mixture to a previously greased baking dish. Pour the whisked eggs over it. Bake for 35 minutes. Enjoy garnished with fresh parsley.

Nutrition: Calories 289, Protein 19.8g Fat 19.7g Carbs 6.3g Sugar 2.4g

38. Keto Tacos with Bacon Sauce

Preparation Time: 30 minutes

Cooking Time: 40 minutes

Servings: 4

Ingredients

- 1 ½ cups ground beef
- 2 jalapeno peppers, minced
- 2 Campari tomatoes, crushed
- 1/2 teaspoon ground cumin
- 6 slices bacon, chopped
- 2 teaspoon champagne vinegar
- 1/2 teaspoon onion powder
- 1/2 teaspoon celery salt
- 1 ½ cups Cotija cheese, shredded
- Salt and ground black pepper, to taste
- 1/2 cup bone broth
- 3 tablespoons tomato paste

Directions

1. Begin by preheating your oven to 3900F. Spritz a baking pan with the aid of a nonstick cooking spray.
2. Spread 6 (sixpiles of Cotija cheese on the baking pan; bake for about 15 minutes; allow taco shells to cool down for some minutes.
3. In a nonstick skillet, brown the beef for the duration of about 4 to 5 minutes crumbling with a spatula. Include crushed pepper, tomatoes, salt, celery salt, onion powder, and ground cumin.

4. Heat until everything is cooked through.
5. Now, make the sauce by cooking the bacon for the duration of 2 to 3 minutes stirring continually. Include the remaining ingredients and heat until everything comes together.
6. After the above, assemble your tacos. Share the meat mixture among 6 taco shells; top with the bacon sauce. Bon appétit!

Nutrition: Calories 258, Protein 16.3g, Fat 19.3g, Carbs 5g, Sugar 2.9g

SOUP AND SALAD

39. Moroccan-Spiced Cauliflower Salad

Preparation Time: 5 minutes

Cooking Time: 25 minutes, plus 15 minutes to cool

Servings: 4

Ingredients:

- 4 cups fresh or frozen cauliflower florets
- 2 tablespoons coconut oil, melted
- 1 teaspoon salt, divided
- ¼ cup extra-virgin olive oil
- Grated zest and juice of 1 lemon
- 1 teaspoon chili powder
- 1 teaspoon ground cinnamon
- 1 teaspoon garlic powder
- ½ teaspoon ground turmeric
- ½ teaspoon ground ginger
- 2 celery stalks, thinly sliced
- ½ cup finely sliced fresh mint
- ¼ cup finely sliced red onion
- ¼ cup shelled pistachios

Directions:

1. If using frozen cauliflower, thaw to room temperature in a colander, draining off any excess water. Cut larger florets into bite-size pieces.

2. Preheat the oven to 450°F and line a baking sheet with aluminum foil.
3. In a medium bowl, toss the cauliflower with coconut oil and ½ teaspoon of salt. Arrange the cauliflower in a single layer on the prepared baking sheet, reserving the seasoned bowl.
4. Roast the cauliflower for 20 to 25 minutes, until it is lightly browned and crispy.
5. While the cauliflower roasts, in the reserved bowl, whisk together the olive oil, lemon zest and juice, the remaining ½ teaspoon of salt, the chili powder, cinnamon, garlic powder, turmeric, and ginger. Stir in the celery, mint, and onion.
6. When the cauliflower is done roasting, remove from the oven and allow to cool for 10 to 15 minutes.
7. Toss the warm (but not too hot) cauliflower with the dressing until well combined. Add the pistachios and toss to incorporate. Serve warm or chilled.

Nutrition: Calories: 262; Total Fat: 24g; Total Carbs: 11g; Net Carbs: 7g; Fiber: 4g; Protein: 4g; Sodium: 651mg; Macros: Fat: 82%, Carbs: 12%, Protein: 6%

40. Creamy Riced Cauliflower Salad

Preparation Time: 10 minutes, plus 30 minutes to chill

Cooking Time: 0 minutes

Servings: 4

Ingredients:

- 4 ounces crumbled sheep's milk feta cheese
- ½ cup Anti-Inflammatory Mayo
- Grated zest and juice of 1 lemon
- 2 tablespoons minced red onion
- 1½ teaspoons dried dill
- ½ teaspoon salt
- 1 teaspoon red pepper flakes, or to taste
- 3 cups fresh riced cauliflower (not frozen)
- ½ cup coarsely chopped pitted Kalamata olives

Directions:

1. In a medium bowl, combine the feta, mayo, lemon zest and juice, onion, dill, salt, and red pepper flakes. Whisk well with a fork until smooth and creamy.
2. Add the cauliflower and olives and mix well to combine.
3. Refrigerate for at least 30 minutes before serving.

Nutrition: Calories: 370; Total Fat: 37g; Total Carbs: 6g; Net Carbs: 4g; Fiber: 2g; Protein: 7g; Sodium: 1048mg; Macros: Fat: 90%, Carbs: 2%, Protein: 8%

41. Loaded Miso Soup with Tofu and Egg

Preparation Time: 10 minutes

Cooking Time: 20 minutes

Servings: 4

Ingredients:

- 3 cups water
- 3 cups vegetable broth
- 3 tablespoons white miso paste
- 1 (2-inch) piece fresh ginger, peeled and minced
- 4 baby bok choy, trimmed and quartered
- 2 cups thinly sliced shiitake mushrooms
- 2 garlic cloves, very thinly sliced
- 1 (14-ounce) package firm tofu, drained and cut into bite-size cubes
- 2 cups spiralized or thinly sliced zucchini
- 2 large hard-boiled eggs, peeled and quartered
- 2 nori seaweed sheets, cut into very thin 2-inch strips
- ¼ cup avocado or extra-virgin olive oil
- 2 teaspoons toasted sesame oil

Directions:

1. In a large saucepan, bring the water and vegetable broth to a boil over high heat. Reduce the heat to low, whisk in the miso paste and ginger, cover and simmer for 2 minutes.
2. Add the bok choy, mushrooms, and garlic. Simmer, covered, for 5 minutes, or until the vegetables are

tender. Remove from the heat and stir in the tofu and zucchini.

3. Divide the mixture between bowls. Add 2 egg quarters and the seaweed strips to each bowl. Drizzle 1 tablespoon of avocado oil and ½ teaspoon of sesame oil over each bowl. Serve warm.

Nutrition: Calories: 378; Total Fat: 29g; Total Carbs: 14g; Net Carbs: 8g; Fiber: 6g; Protein: 17g; Sodium: 912mg; Macros: Fat: 69%, Carbs: 13%, Protein: 18%

42. Weekday Omega-3 Salad

Preparation Time: 10 minutes

Cooking Time: 0 minutes

Servings: 2

Ingredients:

- 6 cups baby arugula or spinach
- 1 (4-ounce) can olive oil–packed tuna, mackerel, or salmon
- ¼ cup minced fresh parsley
- 10 green or black olives, pitted and halved
- 2 tablespoons minced scallions, white and green parts, or red onion
- 1 avocado, thinly sliced
- ¼ cup roasted pumpkin or sunflower seeds
- 6 tablespoons Basic Vinaigrette or Caesar Dressing

Directions:

1. Divide the greens between bowls.
2. In a small bowl, combine the tuna and its oil with the parsley, olives, and scallions. Divide the fish mixture evenly on top of the greens.
3. Divide the avocado slices and pumpkin seeds between the bowls. Drizzle each with the dressing and toss to coat.

Nutrition: Calories: 716; Total Fat: 61g; Total Carbs: 16g; Net Carbs: 5g; Fiber: 11g; Protein: 31g; Sodium: 1021mg; Macros: Fat: 77%, Carbs: 6%, Protein: 17%

43. Classic Coleslaw

Preparation Time: 15 minutes, plus 30 minutes to chill

Cooking Time: 0 minutes

Servings: 4

Ingredients:

- ½ cup Anti-Inflammatory Mayo
- 1 tablespoon avocado or extra-virgin olive oil
- 1 tablespoon Dijon mustard
- 1 tablespoon freshly squeezed lemon juice or apple cider vinegar
- 1 teaspoon salt
- ½ teaspoon ground turmeric
- ½ teaspoon freshly ground black pepper
- 3 cups shredded green cabbage
- 1 cup shredded red cabbage
- 1 cup coarsely chopped baby spinach leaves
- ½ cup chopped fresh cilantro, basil, or parsley
- ¼ small red onion, thinly sliced
- ¼ cup roasted pumpkin seeds or slivered almonds

Directions:

1. In a small bowl, whisk together the mayo, avocado oil, mustard, lemon juice, salt, turmeric, and pepper. Set aside.
2. In a large bowl, combine the green and red cabbages, spinach, cilantro, and red onion. Add the dressing and toss to coat well. Refrigerate for at least 30 minutes to allow flavors to develop.

3. Serve chilled, topped with the pumpkin seeds.

Nutrition: Calories: 349; Total Fat: 35g; Total Carbs: 7g; Net Carbs: 4g; Fiber: 3g; Protein: 4g; Sodium: 856mg; Macros: Fat: 90%, Carbs: 5%, Protein: 5%

44. Weeknight Greek Salad

Preparation Time: 5 minutes

Cooking Time: 0 minutes

Servings: 4

Ingredients:

- 8 cups coarsely chopped romaine lettuce
- 4 ounces crumbled sheep's milk feta cheese
- ½ cup Marinated Antipasto Veggies or store-bought marinated artichoke hearts
- 20 Kalamata olives, pitted
- 2 tablespoons chopped fresh oregano or rosemary, or 2 teaspoons dried oregano
- ¼ cup extra-virgin olive oil
- Juice of 1 lemon
- ½ teaspoon freshly ground black pepper

Directions:

1. In a large bowl, combine the lettuce, feta, antipasto veggies, olives, and oregano. Drizzle with the olive oil, then add the lemon juice and pepper. Toss to coat and serve immediately.

Nutrition: Calories: 300; Total Fat: 27g; Total Carbs: 10g; Net Carbs: 7g; Fiber: 3g; Protein: 6g; Sodium: 795mg; Macros: Fat: 81%, Carbs: 11%, Protein: 8%

45. Italian Green Bean Salad

Preparation Time: 5 minutes

Cooking Time: 5 minutes, plus 1 hour to chill

Servings: 4

Ingredients:

- ¼ cup extra-virgin olive oil, divided
- 1 pound green beans, trimmed
- 2 tablespoons red wine vinegar
- 1 teaspoon salt
- 1 teaspoon red pepper flakes
- 2 garlic cloves, thinly sliced
- ½ cup slivered almonds
- ¼ cup thinly sliced fresh basil
- 2 tablespoons chopped fresh mint

Directions:

1. In a large skillet, heat 2 tablespoons of olive oil over medium-high heat. Add the green beans and sauté for about 5 minutes, until they are just tender. Remove from the heat and transfer to a large serving bowl.

2. In a small bowl, whisk together the remaining 2 tablespoons of olive oil, the vinegar, salt, red pepper flakes, and garlic. Pour the dressing over the green beans and toss to coat well.

3. Add the almonds, basil, and mint and toss well. Serve warm or chill for at least 1 hour to serve cold.

Nutrition: Calories: 238; Total Fat: 21g; Total Carbs: 12g; Net Carbs: 7g; Fiber: 5g; Protein: 5g; Sodium: 598mg; Macros: Fat: 79%, Carbs: 13%, Protein: 8

SNACK

46. Saucy Brussels sprouts and Carrots

Preparation Time: 15 minutes

Cooking Time: 12 minutes

Servings: 4

Ingredients:

- 1 tablespoon coconut oil
- 12 ounces Brussels sprouts, tough ends removed and cut in half
- 12 ounces carrots (about 4 medium), peeled, ends removed, and cut into 1" chunks
- ¼ cup fresh lime juice
- ¼ cup apple cider vinegar
- ½ cup coconut amino
- ¼ cup almond butter

Directions:

1. Sauté the Brussels sprouts and carrots and sauté until browned, about 5–7 minutes.
2. While the vegetables are browning, make the sauce. Mix the lime juice, vinegar, coconut amino, and almond butter in a small bowl.
3. Pour the sauce over the vegetables—Cook within 6 minutes. Serve.

Nutrition: Calories: 216 Fat: 11g Protein: 6g Sodium: 738mg
Fiber: 6g Carbohydrates: 22g Sugar: 5g

47. Steamed Purple Sweet Potatoes

Preparation Time: 5 minutes

Cooking Time: 40 minutes

Servings: 4

Ingredients:

- 4 purple sweet potatoes, whole and unpeeled

Directions:

1. Place in a steamer basket and steam until thoroughly cooked, approximately 40 minute.

Nutrition: Energy (calories): 762 kcal Protein: 45.18 g Fat: 9.25 g Carbohydrates: 160.03 g

48. Mexican Veggie Meat

Preparation Time: 10 minutes

Cooking Time: 0 minutes

Servings: 4

Ingredients:

- 2 cups sunflower seeds, soaked 8 hours and rinsed
- 5 cups zucchini, shredded
- 1/2 cup onion, minced
- 1 cup celery, minced
- 1/2 cup homemade chili powder
- 1/4 cup lemon juice
- 1 teaspoon unrefined salt
- 2 garlic cloves, crushed

Directions:

1. Use a food processor to process sunflower seeds into flour.
2. In a large bowl, combine with other ingredients.
3. Spread the mixture onto two dehydrator sheets lined with parchment paper.
4. Dehydrate at 109 degrees F for 5 hours (or until it reaches your desired consistency).

Nutrition: Energy (calories): 2132 kcal Protein: 80.1 g Fat: 163.49 g Carbohydrates: 153.89 g

49. Flaxseed Crackers

Preparation Time: 10 minutes

Cooking Time: 0 minutes

Servings: 3

Ingredients:

- 2 cups flax seeds (soaked for 1-2 hours in 2 cups of water)
- 1/3 Cup red bell pepper, chopped finely
- 2/3 Cup sun dried tomatoes
- 1/3 Cup fresh cilantro or basil, chopped finely
- 1 ¼ cups tomatoes, diced
- 1 clove garlic, minced
- Pinch cayenne
- 1 teaspoon unrefined salt

Directions:

1. Place bell pepper, cilantro, sun dried tomatoes, tomatoes, cayenne, garlic, and salt into food processor and process until pureed.
2. Transfer contents into a large bowl and mix in the flax seeds.
3. Spread mixture onto a dehydrator sheet and dehydrate at 109 degrees F for about 18 hours.

Nutrition: Energy (calories): 1774 kcal Protein: 65.67 g Fat: 145.63 g Carbohydrates: 86.04 g

50. Buckwheat Crackers

Preparation Time: 10 minutes

Cooking Time: 0 minutes

Servings: 4

Ingredients:

- 1½ cups raw buckwheat groats, sprouted 2 days and rinsed
- 1 small bell pepper
- ½ zucchini
- 1 cup of young coconut meat. (This requires 1-2 young coconuts)
- ½ teaspoon unrefined salt.
- 1 teaspoon dried basil (optional)
- ¼ teaspoon dried oregano (optional)

Directions:

1. Pulse buckwheat groats in food processor. The groats should be coarsely chopped and not overly processed.
2. Place the processed groats into a large bowl.
3. Quarter the bell pepper and cut zucchini into smaller pieces before placing into processor.
4. In the food processor, pulse the bell pepper and zucchini into finely chopped pieces (doing your best not to puree the mixture) and add it to the bowl when done.
5. Process coconut meat very thoroughly and add it to the bowl.
6. Mix all ingredients well.

7. Spread onto dehydrator trays lined with parchment paper.
8. Dehydrate at 109 degrees F for about 18 hours. Crackers should be very dry without a hint of moisture or softness.
9. Use in place of bread for lunch.
10. Top with avocado slices and a pinch of salt.

Nutrition: Energy (calories): 268 kcal Protein: 6.21 g Fat: 14.25 g Carbohydrates: 33.7 g

DESSERTS

51. Pineapple Pie

Preparation Time: 15 minutes

Cooking Time: 50 minutes

Servings: 8

Ingredients:

- 5-Tbsps raw honey (divided)
- 15-pcs sweet cherries, fresh or frozen
- 2-pcs fresh pineapple, peeled, cored, and sliced into rings
- 3-Tbsps liquid coconut oil
- 2-pcs eggs
- 1-tsp pure vanilla extract
- 1-cup almond flour
- ½-tsp baking powder

Directions:

1. Preheat your oven to 350 ℉.
2. Pour 1½-tablespoon of the honey in a round baking tin. Arrange the cherries and pineapple rings on the bed of honey in a decorative pattern. Put the pan in the oven, and bake for 15 minutes.
3. In the meantime, stir in all the remaining ingredients in a mixing bowl. Mix well until forming the mixture into dough. Set aside.

4. Take the pan out from the oven. Press down the batter over the pineapple rings, smoothing it at the top.
5. Return the pan in the oven, and bake further for 35 minutes.

Nutrition: Calories: 213 | Fat: 7.1g | Protein: 15.9g | Sodium: 39.2mg | Total Carbs: 23.7g | Dietary Fiber: 2.4g | Net Carbs: 21.3g

52. Citrus Cauliflower Cake

Preparation Time: 5-hours 30-minutes

Cooking Time: 0 minutes

Servings: 10

Ingredients:

- For the Crust:
- 2½-cups pecan nuts
- 1-cup dates, pitted
- 2-Tbsps maple syrup or agave
- For the Filling:
- 3-pcs avocados, halved and pitted
- 3-cups cauliflower, riced
- 1½-cups pineapple, crushed
- ¾-cup maple syrup or agave
- 1-pc lemon, zest and juice
- A pinch of cinnamon
- ½-tsp lemon extract
- ½-tsp pure vanilla extract
- For the Topping:
- 3-Tbsps maple syrup or agave
- 1-tsp pure vanilla extract
- 1½-cups plain coconut yogurt

Directions:

1. For the Crust:
2. Line a baking tray with parchment paper. Set the outer ring of a 9-inch spring-form pan onto the baking tray.

3. Pulse the pecans in your food processor to a finely ground texture. Add the remaining crust ingredients, and pulse further until the mixture holds together.
4. Transfer and press the mixture to an even layer in the baking tray.
5. For the Filling:
6. Wipe the bowl of your food processor, and add in the avocado, cauliflower, pineapple, syrup, and lemon zest and juice. Process the mixture to a smooth consistency.
7. Add the cinnamon and the lemon and vanilla extracts. Pulse until thoroughly combined. Pour the mixture over the crust. Place the tray in your freezer overnight, or for 5 hours.
8. Take the cake out from your freezer, and let it sit at room temperature for 20 minutes. Remove the outer ring.
9. For the Topping:
10. Stir in all the topping ingredients in a mixing bowl. Pour the mixture over the cake and spread evenly.

Nutrition: Calories: 667 Fat: 22.2g Protein: 33.3g Sodium: 237mg Total Carbs: 88.1g Dietary Fiber: 4.8g Net Carbs: 83.3g

53. Sweet Strawberry Sorbet

Preparation Time: 5 minutes

Cooking Time: 0 minutes

Servings: 3

Ingredients:

- 1-lb strawberries, frozen
- 1-cup orange juice or 1-cup coconut water

Directions:

1. Process the strawberries in your food processor for 2 minutes, or until the fruit turns into flakes. Pour the orange juice, and process further into a smooth frozen puree.
2. To serve, you may present it either as a chilled soft dessert or as sorbet, frozen after an hour and 45 minutes. You can also serve it like a Popsicle by pouring the soft serve into Popsicle molds and freezing overnight.

Nutrition: Calories: 86 Fat: 2.3g Protein: 5.3g Sodium: 7mg Total Carbs: 20.3g Dietary Fiber: 9.6g Net Carbs: 10.7g

54. Creamy & Chilly Blueberry Bites

Preparation Time: 2-hours 5-minutes

Cooking Time: 0 minutes

Servings: 2

Ingredients:

- 1-pint blueberries
- 2-tsps lemon juice
- 8-oz. vanilla yogurt

Directions:

1. Coat the blueberries with the lemon juice and yogurt in a mixing bowl. Toss carefully without squishing the berries.
2. Scoop out each of the coated berries and place them on a baking sheet lined with parchment paper. Put the sheet in your freezer for two hours before serving.

Nutrition: Calories: 394 Fat: 13.1g Protein: 19.7g Sodium: 164mg Total Carbs: 58.9g Dietary Fiber: 9.7g Net Carbs: 49.2g

55. Pistachioed Panna-Cotta Cocoa

Preparation Time: 18 minutes

Cooking Time: 2 minutes

Servings: 6

Ingredients:

- 12-oz. dark chocolate
- 1-Tbsp coconut oil
- 3-pcs large bananas, sliced into thirds
- Cocoa nibs, chopped
- Spiced or smoked almonds, chopped
- Salted pistachios, chopped

Directions:

1. Line a baking pan with parchment paper.
2. Melt the dark chocolate with oil in your microwave. Set aside.
3. Pierce a Popsicle stick halfway into one end of each banana.
4. Dip each banana into the melted chocolate. Place dipped bananas into the baking sheet. Sprinkle generously with the cocoa nibs, almonds, and pistachios. Place the sheet in your freezer to harden and set.

Nutrition: Calories: 454 Fat: 15.1g Protein: 22.7g Sodium: 91mg Total Carbs: 61.6g Dietary Fiber: 4.9g Net Carbs: 56.7g

CONCLUSION:

Diet is a major cause of inflammation and long-term health problems. A great diet can significantly reduce your risk of stroke, heart disease, arthritis, diabetes and many other diseases. Unfortunately, it is not as simple as eating a few vegetables and fish regularly. There are a variety of factors that influence how your body handles your food, so it's important to stay on top of things. If you're making healthy eating changes, then you have to be sure to keep healthy eating habits in your day-to-day life as well.

The Anti-inflammatory Anti-Inflammation Diet Cookbook is designed to help you make the best decisions for managing your diet on the Anti-inflammatory Anti-Inflammation Diet.

It's important to choose the right nutrition when you're fighting inflammation in the body. Here are some simple diet tips that can help you have your best day yet!

Drink lots of water. Chronic dehydration can cause inflammation. You should try to drink at least two liters of water a day. If you're sick, drink even more to make yourself feel better!

Eat anti-inflammatory foods. The best way to fight inflammation is to eat foods that support your body's ability to heal. Try some omega-3 fatty acids, which can reduce inflammation and soothe joint pain. Also, eating foods rich in antioxidants, like blueberries and bell peppers, will give your body the support it needs to fight inflammation.

Exercise. This can be the best ways to relieve joint pain. Jogging, walking, and using an exercise machine can help keep your joints healthy and strong! Don't exercise too much though; if you're not used to it, you could get sore faster than usual. Use common sense when figuring out how much exercise you need to be healthy! You can talk to your doctor about how much you should be exercising each day, but remember: Exercise is great for relieving joint pain!

CPSIA information can be obtained
at www.ICGtesting.com
Printed in the USA
BVHW041350200421
605393BV00001B/109